Kindle Fire Tips and Tricks

James Avery

CONTENTS

INTRODUCTION

When Amazon introduced Kindle Fire, a multitude of people were delighted. Finally, a tablet that performs well and is affordable at the same time. While the original Kindle fire was a functional device, what made it worth all the hassle was that it was very affordable. Anybody lusting after an iPad but not being able to master the courage to buy one because of the price finally had some reprieve. Kindle fire was and still is a gadget for the masses.

Its successor on the other hand, Kindle Fire HD, is a device to marvel at. It is slightly more expensive than its predecessor, $299 for 16GB whereas Kindle Fire was under $200, (not by much, it was $199, but under $200 none the less). Which is to be expected, after all, this is a much better version than the original Kindle Fire. Let's take a quick tour of the Kindle Fire HD and see what makes it such a bargain.

Kindle Fire HD doesn't vary that much from its predecessor in terms of design. They both look and even feel the same, only this newer version is slightly bigger. It of course has an 8.9" screen whereas its predecessor had 7". This means that the dimensions of the Kindle Fire HD are going to be slightly different to make room for the improvement. It measures 240 x 165mm (9.45 x 6.5") and is slightly heavier than the 7" model (It weighs 20 ounces whereas the 7" model weighs only 13.9 ounces). The redeeming factor is that it is actually thinner than the original, 0.35" to the original 0.4". Not much of a difference but it is very noticeable. The design remains refreshingly similar only this version is darker and slightly glossier.

As much as it might not be the fastest machine on the planet, it certainly holds its own when it comes to performance. It has a 512MB RAM, with a 1GHz dual-core CPU. The on-board storage capacity is 8GB while its Wi-Fi is 802.11b/g/n. It has a set of rather powerful stereo speakers at the back. The sound is reasonable enough but you might just want to plug it into an external device like maybe your home theater or a set of heavy duty headphones. Seeing as you only get 8GB of on-board storage, you are probably going to be limited to simply streaming, which it does wonderfully, but the limited storage bit might be a problem for some people.

It has a 1024 x 600 LCD display that works rather well with all types of media. The touch response performs well and the display captures pictures and texts in a very refreshing crisp manner.

Amazon said that the battery life on their device could go up to 8 hours without charging. This is true, the battery performs very well. And as far as performance is concerned, Amazon's Kindle Fire and Kindle Fire HD can hold their own in this android arena. There are something's that Amazon should probably look into, like making it possible for their users to tell what the battery life without having to go into the settings menu, but all in all, it performs at par with its competitors.

Kindle Fire HD is a definite step up from its predecessor, although not by much. It runs the same user interface only this time it has better responsiveness and usability.

Pitted against its competition like the Nexus 7, you could probably argue that Kindle Fire 7" was neck to neck with the other players. Of course when Kindle Fire HD was introduced, many people expected more of a fight from Amazon. The 8.9" definitely holds its own when it comes to performance and display in comparison to its competition, but as far as it's comparison to its predecessor is concerned, it all just a little bit of a step up.

Slightly better performance, a slightly better look and feel as well as cellular connectivity and size. Amazon has done a lot to be recognized as a major contender in the android arena. If these are signs of things to come, then the competition better consider themselves put on notice, Amazon is coming and they are coming fast. Hopefully the Kindle Fire 7 and Kindle Fire HD will not be the last we see of tablets from Amazon.

So how can you get more from your kindle fire and fire HD? In this guidebook you'll find tons of tips, tricks, shortcuts, FAQ's on how to protect your device, become more productive and ways to save a small fortune with totally free apps.

James Avery.

KINDLE FIRE BATTERY FAQ'S

How Do I Charge The Battery On A Kindle Fire?

Charging the Kindle Fire is an easy task for users, similar to the way used for charging cell phones, simply connect the power adapter of your Kindle Fire (one end to your wall socket and another end to your device) and your battery will start charging.

If all of this is done properly you should see the light on your Kindle light up when it is charging. If you find the light not working, you will need to check power adapter to ensure the line is okay. When you see the orange light come on (which is located near the cable connection) your device will start to charge.

How Long Does The Kindle Fire Battery Last?

The life of a Kindle Fire battery will depend on how much or how many activities are running on your Kindle after it's been charged. The Kindle Fire is powered by Li Polymer Battery, which should provide up to 8 hours of use. Although this may be reduced if you use too many energy consuming apps or software that's running at the same time.

Why Does My Kindle Battery Run Out Even When It's Not Being Used?

Kindle Fires often lose battery power even when it's not being used by the user. This can come about due to the Kindle Fire needing time to switch off. This is one of the prime reasons which users find their battery life depleted when they try to start it up again. To prevent this the user needs to turn off the device fully which can be done by holding the power button for around 30 seconds to make sure it turns off completely.

How Can I Extend My Kindle Fire's Battery Life?

Here are some ways to optimize the settings to boost the battery life of your Kindle Fire-

1. <u>Turn off the Wi-Fi Feature</u>- If you do not need to use the Wireless network on your Kindle Fire, you need to turn off this feature. Whenever you need to use the Wi-Fi again, you can turn on it and off through the settings in the settings bar at the top of the screen.

2. <u>Keep Your Kindle Fire in Sleep Mode</u>- The battery life will always remain in use when your Kindle Fire is running. However, you can reduce this by putting your Kindle Fire in sleep mode.

3. <u>Modify Brightness Levels</u>- Due to the Kindle Fire screen size, screen brightness is the main thing which eats up your battery life. Thus to save battery life, you should change or reduce your brightness screen levels to increase battery life. To do this go to the setting bar at the top of the screen and reduce brightness levels.

4. <u>Delete Battery Hungry Apps</u>- There are some apps in your Kindle store and available online which can eat up your battery life. If you find your battery draining quickly using certain apps, (which seem energy intensive) it's best to delete them or use them only when needed.

How Long Does It Take To Charge A Kindle Fire Battery?

The Kindle Fire battery life is usually depleted within 8 hours of normal use. To charge your Kindle Fire it can take 4 hours of continuous charging. For faster charging times its best to order a power fast adapter to speed up the process - http://amzn.to/18CW1NF

How Can I Tell If My Kindle Fire Is Charging?

There are two lights on the Kindle Fire which are an "Orange" and "Green" color. When you plug-in your battery charger to your device, the orange color light will turn on. This is the sign that your Kindle Fire is now successfully charging.

What If The Screen Is Blank, How Can I Tell If It's Charging?

When your screen is blank, try to turn on your Kindle by pressing the power button and turn on your Kindle. The Kindle should show you the charging logo when you will start this, however if your battery is very depleted and the logo hasn't appeared, the best way is to check your Kindle Fire's "orange power light" is on.

KINDLE FIRE SETTINGS FAQ'S

The Kindle Fire Screen Settings - How Do I Change The Settings To Suit Me?

To access the setting on your Kindle Fire, place your finger on the very top edge of the screen and swipe downwards. This will cause a pop up window to appear that gives direct access to the most frequently needed settings. The Kindle Fire screen have lots of different settings options which give you different looks and options when you will change your settings accordingly.

Here are some of the commonly asked setting question...

How Do I Set A Screen Lock Password? – For security reasons you can easily set any password to restrict access to your Kindle Fire without your permission. Through the settings, you can restrict others from using your Kindle in your absence. To set a screen password, you have to go Security tab and enter your lock screen password (a 4-character password of your choice) to lock your screen. To remove this restriction, go to the Security tab again and then choose to stop this.

How Do I Change The Device's Language? - The Kindle Fire normally always comes to the user with English Language as default however if you are from any other country, you may need to change the language to French, German, Italian, Spanish or Japanese. To do this swipe down, tap "More" and select "Language & Keyboard" to change the language. Then, click on Language and select the language that you prefer.

How Do I Change the Device's Time? - When you first set up your Kindle Fire or enter into new time zone, you need to set the time accordingly. To do this swipe down from the screen's top edge and choose the "More" tab and then select the "Date & Time" option. Select your Time Zone and press okay to select your time zone correctly.

KINDLE FIRE CAROUSEL FAQ'S

The Carousel on the Kindle Fire home screen is one the areas of your Kindle you'll be coming back to again and again. This is the place where you'll find the shortcuts to your recently used apps and other files you commonly use. You can customize this area and place the shortcuts that suit you within easy reach for when you need them. Having the carousel on your Kindle Fire, means you can go to your favorite apps within a moment notice and avoid having to search to find them.

How Do I Delete Apps from the Carousel, Tidy Them Up And Add Them To My Favorites List?

To Remove An APP

- To remove an app from your home screen, you need to do some steps. To remove an app from the carousel, place and hold your finger (without taking it off) on the app image shortcut until the "Remove" tab appears. You now have the option of deleting the app from either the carousel or deleting it completely from the device.

- Or another option of deleting an app is to go to "Settings", go to "More" tab and then select "Applications". Then, tap down the list and select App Manager and select "Clear Data". You will now have removed the app from your home screen.

To Remove A Web Page

- To remove web pages from your carousel home screen, you need to open the "Web" tab and go to the "Menu" icon and then go to "Settings". In this setting list you'll find the "Clear History" option, select this and it will remove all "Web Pages" from your home screen.

- You can also use the option of holding your finger on the web page "Icon" on the home screen carousel until the delete pop up message appears and then select remove from carousel.

To Add An App To Your Favorites List

You can also add your favorite apps, videos, web pages or music tracks to your favorites list so they can be launched quickly without having to do a search for them. To add any particular object to your favorites list, click and hold down the app, book, webpage icon until the small pop up message appears. Then select the "Add to favorite" option. Your app is now in your favorites list, which can be found by taping the "*" symbol at the bottom right hand side of the Kindle Fire carousel home screen.

If My Screen Freezes What Do I Do?

There will be times when you may notice a lag time in your screen and it may seem to freeze while playing an app. If your screen freezes, try leaving it alone for a moment before trying out a solution to fix it. If things haven't rectified themselves after a minute or so, a normal restart should sort this problem out and thing will go back to normal. If this happens regularly with a particular app, its best to delete this app or see it there's an update available that may sort out this problem.

What's Best For Cleaning The Screen On A Kindle Fire?

When it comes to cleaning the screen on your kindle fire, it pays to only use safe cleaning options on your screen. Please be aware that this chapter is only a guideline for the user and at all costs do not, repeat do not use any harsh or abrasive chemicals compounds that may scratch or damage your screen. As always when buying any computer screen cleaning spray and wipes, you should read the instructions and that make sure they're always right for the job.

With that advice out of the way, here are some screen solutions you can try out…

Screen Clear 2goTM Organic Digital Cleaning Kit - Screen Clear 2goTM Organic Digital Cleaning Kit is perfect for anyone who owns lots of touch screen devices such as Kindles, cell phones and tablets. SC2G provides a safe way to clean the Kindle Fire's screen and is free from any types of chemicals that can damage your screen's condition. The product is also verified and tested by the environment testing laboratory.

Moshi Teraglove Screen Cleaner For Kindle Fire

Moshi Teraglove Screen Cleaner for Kindle Fire is specially made for touch screen device and is a cleaner that's created in the shape of a glove with microfiber attached. This allows the easy removal of dust, fingerprints and grease from your display and give you back a clear screen. http://amzn.to/18GFzzo

M&S ScreenCleen SC44215 Mini Cleaning Canister

M&S ScreenCleen SC44215 is a mini Canister filled with cleaning wipes (similar to baby wipes) that can be used on touch screen devices like the Kindle Fire. Each wipe contains a small amount to cleaning fluid that can safely clean your touch screen of dust etc. Each canister provides 15 wipes and can be bought as a six pack. http://amzn.to/19lUzBW

Screen Protectors Are They Any Good And Where Can I Buy Them?

Having any type of tablet device with a touch screen means it's important to protect it, and one of those ways is with a screen protector. Between falls and damage by small children it can be costly to have to buy a replacement screen. With that in mind here's some ways of protecting your Kindle Fire's screen…

Moshi iVisor AG Screen Protection for Kindle Fire (Anti-Glare)

Moshi iVisor AG Screen Protection for Kindle Fire (Anti-Glare) is screen protector that is easy to use and install on your Kindle Fire screen (although not available for Kindle Fire HD). It doesn't take long to install and helps to reduce screen glare. The EZ-Glide surface technology of this protective shield also allows you to still use the touch screen properly. This protector also helps reduce smudging of fingerprint and protects your device from any type of scratch damage. http://amzn.to/13hQ3wR

Belkin Screen Protector for Kindle Fire - 4 Pack

Belkin Screen Protector for Kindle Fire is another useful protector for your device to prevent scratches and oils and grease from fingers to build up on the screen. There's also a smoothing card included with this product to helps adhere the protector to the screen and prevent any air bubbles becoming trapped underneath. This product comes both with a warranty, four screen protective shield including overlays, smoothing card, cleaning wipe and dust revival included in each pack. http://amzn.to/15PLhZS

KINDLE FIRE KEYBOARD FAQ'S

How Do I Change The Settings On A Kindle Fire Keyboard?

To find the settings for the Kindle Fire go to the settings options and choose keyboard settings. There you can find whatever settings you need to make to the keyboard to suit you. Apart from changing the Kindle fire keyboard settings there also some commonly used shortcuts that can speed up your productivity.

Here's a list of the most commonly used functions on the Kindle Fire Keyboard…

Keyboard Shortcut	What it does
Alt+B	Sets or removes a bookmark
Alt+G	Refreshes the screen
Alt+F	Skips to the next MP3
Alt+spacebar	Plays or stops MP3s
Back button	Turns off Text-to-Speech
Spacebar	Spacebar
Shift+Sym	Turns on Text-to-Speech
Menu button	Displays the time and available memory
Alt+Home	Goes to the Kindle Store

HOW TO PROTECT YOUR KINDLE FIRE

Protecting your Kindle Fire should be upmost in your mind, not only can a physical drop or scratch cause damage to your Kindle Fire you also need to protect the contents of your Kindle Fire. As most of us know nowadays emails, private documents, photo's or credit card details getting in the wrong hands can be worse than any physical damage. With that in mind here's some way of improving the security of your Kindle Fire…

1. **Lock It**- Locking a Kindle Fire with a strong password is a great deterrent to preventing anyone getting into the contents of your device.

2. **Lock Down Your WI-Fi**- When protecting your Kindle Fire, you should use any password protection for the Wi-Fi connection of your home. This way anyone uses your Kindle Fire, he or she can't get access to the web without permission. This way you can protect your children from content that you don't want them to see. This can also stop any in app purchases from happening which can quickly deplete any funds you may have on a debit or credit card.

3. **Clean Up the Browser History**- When using any Web Browser for browsing the internet, you should always delete cookies, clear the cache, clear the history as well as clear your saved passwords. This way you won't have to worry about any of your browsing history getting in the wrong hands.

How To Protect Yourself In Free WiFi Areas

Sometimes that free WiFi in the local coffee shop can be very costly. So to protect your Kindle Fire and kindle passwords from snoopers, it's important to get out of the habit of saving passwords to important websites like banking sites when using free WiFi. These passwords getting into the wrong hands can be very costly compared to that cup of coffee.

Protecting Your Kindle Fire

Now that we've got the security protection of Kindle Fire sorted, how can you protect your kindle from physical damage? Without protecting your Kindle Fire a drop, even a small one, can lead to a costly repair bill. Here are some tips to extend the life of your Kindle Fire so that you can use it for a long time to come.

Secure Screen Protector- Using a transparent screen protector on your screen is a great way of protecting your touch screen from wear and tear and reducing fingers and body oils forming on the screen. Some also have an anti-glare property to make it easier to read your Kindle Fire in brighter conditions

Kindle Fire Case- If you want to keep your Kindle Fire damage free during your travel, its best to buy a quality case to protect it. Well-designed cases and covers are now available in lots of materials and colors that now give great external protection from damage.

Avoid High And Low Temperatures – As well as protecting your device's screen and case it's also important to protect the inner workings of the Kindle Fire. Leaving a Kindle Fire in an area where it can experience high and low temperatures may damage internal parts of your device.

HOW TO PUT NON AMAZON FILES ON A KINDLE FIRE

While you might be happy with the great content you can get from the Amazon kindle store there will come a time when you want to put your own content on to your Kindle Fire. Whether that's a document, picture or video it's worth knowing how to do this. While you may need to connect your Kindle Fire to your PC/laptop with a USB cable it can be also be done through email.

Sometimes getting documents on your device is as simple as sending an email to your Kindle Fire. If you've got multiple files they can easily be sent in .Zip format and sent to your Kindle Fire through its unique email address. (To find the email address that's unique to your Kindle Fire, click on the "DOCS" tab at the top of the home screen. Your Kindle Fire's email address is shown under the "Cloud" tab in the format **xxxxxxxx@kindle.com**) Then after you've uploaded the files through email the next step, is to go to the "Sync" option of Kindle Fire and synchronize it. Your new documents will show up in the Doc's section. To view them go to the "Docs" tab at the top of the Kindle Fire home screen to view them. You can then use whatever particular app to open those Docs files. The document file formats that are supported on the Kindle Fire are AZW, TXT,PDF, MOBI, PRC, DOC, DOCX

How do I get PDF's onto my Kindle Fire?

To get PDF files on your Kindle Fire, it's the same as transferring other document files on your Kindle. You may however have to convert the files into real and native PDF format otherwise it won't be supported and you may not be able to open it on your tablet device.

How Do I Get My Music Files To Play On My Kindle Fire?

The music formats supported by the Kindle Fire are MP3, Non-DRM AAC (.m4a), MIDI, OGG, and WAV. In order to get music to play on your Kindle Fire, there are two ways you can do it. First you can use the USB cable that is provided with your Kindle Fire (join it with your computer) and then do a straight transfer to the music folder of your kindle.

Or secondly, you can use the Amazon cloud account to transfers music to your Kindle Fire. To do this you need to go to your Amazon account and upload your music to the Amazon cloud. Once it's in the cloud it's just a simple transfer to your kindle. To play the music, use any music app or player and select your song you'd like to play.

How Do I Put A DVD or Home Movie Onto My Kindle Fire?

In order to put a DVD or home movie on your Kindle Fire, you will need to use the supplied USB cable. Connect the cable with your computer/laptop and then simply transfer them to the movie folder of your Kindle Fire. This is a simple copy/paste job that you would do on other device. Kindle Fire doesn't support all formats of video and is only.to display MP4 and .VP8 formats. If your file differs from these 2 you will need to convert it first.

How Do I Get Rid Of Books That Won't Delete Off My Kindle?

Sometimes you may come across a stubborn book that for some reason just won't delete from your Kindle. To get around this problem you'll need to log into your Amazon account and then go to your e-books library. In this page, you will find your books titles with actions you can do for each book. To delete the problem book use "Actions" tab and then select "Delete from Library" to delete. Then simply sync your Kindle Fire (with the "Sync" option in the kindle home page drop down menu) and this should successfully remove the book once and for all.

KINDLE FIRE HELP AND ADVICE – WHERE SHOULD YOU GO FOR HELP

You may feel like you're the only one in the world with a particular kindle fire problem but there are plenty of solutions online. From Amazon.com to Kindle Fire forums and Facebook groups there's a wealth of knowledge you can call on for help. With that in mind where can you go if something goes wrong...

When facing problems with your Kindle Fire, one of the first places its best to go to is the Amazon website. It's packed with a wealth of questions and answers (provided by both staff and other Kindle Fire users) that cover nearly all of the topics you'd ever need to know. http://amzn.to/16hAhEr

When looking for solutions to your Kindle Fire problems you can also find other Kindle users groups on Facebook. There you can find answers to many Kindle FAQ's, problems and how to get the most from your Kindle Fire. http://on.fb.me/16hAo2V

Websites and forums are also a wealth of knowledge online for help with your Kindle Fire. A simple search on your favorite search engine with the search string "Kindle Fire Forum" or "Kindle Fire Website" will return hundreds if not thousands of places where you can find solutions to the most stubborn or difficult Kindle Fire problems. These sites are not only a wealth of information but you'll always be able to find out the latest news, tips and tricks to getting the most from your Kindle Fire.

And finally, if you're a person who learns better through video rather than text, YouTube is also a great place to find help and advice. Here you find a lots of video's covering tips, advice on changing settings, frequently asked questions, how to unlock, root your Kindle Fire and much more.

WHERE TO FIND FREE KINDLE BOOKS

Finding free books for your Kindle Fire isn't hard if you know where to look. Here are just a small selection of great places online to fill up your kindle with great content…

Amazon.com - Although Amazon is filled with lots of great paid books you can find tons of books that are free of charge. A quick search on Amazon using the "free book" search string will reveal lots of free kindle books just waiting to be read. http://amzn.to/13KmAPz

Pixel of Ink - Pixel of Ink is another website, where you can find lots of Kindle books for users to download free from the website. The website has many books from various niches and categories that are both free and paid. One of the best things for kindle users is all book files are in the Kindle format and don't require any type of book converting software to convert them. http://bit.ly/n73Mdr

BookLending.com - BookLending is a website similar to a public library where you can borrow books to read. To avail of free books you'll need to sign up for an account before you download. http://bit.ly/ikh0WZ

EReaderIQ - eReaderIQ is a fantastic site with lots of great search features, from books for $1 to the most popular free books. You'll find lots of great content to get your hands on here. http://bit.ly/b575MQ

Smashwords.com – While its doesn't have as many free books as other sites there are some free kindle books available to download. http://bit.ly/14dVnkj

What Websites, Facebook Groups, and Twitter Feeds Can I Get Free Kindle Books?

When looking for free Kindle books joining groups on Facebook, twitter and other social groups can make sure you're always in the loop when great Kindle books come available free of charge.

Twitter – To find twitter feeds and followers that advertise free kindle books, search twitter.com using the search keywords "Free Kindle Book"

"Kindle Books" to find out who to follow and where to go to get tons of free Kindle books.

Facebook – Like above the tip above, a quick search on Facebook.com using the keywords "Free kindle book" "Kindle book" or "Kindle" will reveal lots of great places to download free books. It's also a great way to meet other kindle fire users to ask for help if you've got a problem.

When looking for websites for free books, a quick search on Google.com will return a vast list of websites where you can get free Kindle books to download and read.

HOW TO INSTALL NON AMAZON ANDROID APPLICATIONS ON A KINDLE FIRE

The Kindly Fire is one of the best-selling mobile gadgets in the world. This gadget is powered by Android system. However, most of the applications that are compatible for this unit are not for free. This makes it hard for Kindle Fire users to enjoy their portable gadgets as much as they'd like. Fortunately, there are some websites that offer free kindle fire apps. The two most popular sites that provide free Android applications for Kindle fire users are http://www.mobile9.gallery.com and http://m.freefireapps.net

These two websites offer the latest, the hottest, and the most popular free Android applications for the Kindle Fire. There are even several categories to choose from, which means that users can find what really suits their needs. If you own a Kindly Fire unit and you are looking for free applications, then these two websites below will serve as your gateway to lots of great free kindle fire apps.

You can easily download all of the available applications without worrying of about payments. And the apps are freshly designed and free to download for all Android mobile users.

How Can I Download A Free Kindle Fire Application From the Internet For My Kindle Fire?

There are lots of great apps out there but it can be tiresome to find the right application that suits your interests especially at the right price. However sometimes paid doesn't always mean the best. With a little knowledge and work you can find and install some of the best kindle fire apps totally free of charge. All you have to do is to follow these simple instructions to properly download some great android apps to your kindle today.

Instructions for http://www.mobile9.gallery.com:
(Note: Make sure that you are connected to a stable wireless connection to

download the application without technical problems)

1. Go to your settings and activate your "Wi-Fi search" application.

2. Scan for the available Wi-Fi spot.

3. Connect on it. However, if the available Wi-Fi connection requires a password, then you should type in the password first before you will be authenticated and permitted to connect.

4. Once connected, open your kindle fire "internet browser".

5. Key in the link http://www.mobile9.gallery.com

6. Wait until the website is completely loaded.

7. Once on the site, you will be asked if you to optimize the site for mobile or for a desktop version.

8. Choose the mobile version for faster and simple website surface. (However, some models of Kindle Fire are automated with optimizing of the site platform. This will not require you to readjust the configuration of the site).

9. After configuration, you should check the "choose mobile device" tab at the upper portion of the site.

10. Click the tab and scan for "Kindle Fire"

11. Afterwards, you will be redirected to a page with the different models of Kindle Fire.

12. Choose the specific model type of your unit and click it. It redirects you to another page where the free kindle fire apps for your specified model are listed.

13. After loading, you should now check the list of available categories at the right side of the site. In here, there are several categories to choose from. You may notice that there are numbers enclosed in parenthesis right after each category. The indicated numbers represent the quantity of

available free applications on that specific category. For instance, if you see (30) right after the "eBooks" category, it means that there are thirty free eBooks available for your Kindle Fire unit.

14. Click the specific category to view the list of available free applications.

15. In here, you will see several lists of applications that are classified under a specific category. Each application has an image and a short description. There are few reviews, as well. This can help you determine the usability of the application that may suit your specific interest.

16. Once you find the right application, you can click the image or the specific name of the software.

17. There will be new pop-up window that will display the process of downloading the application.

18. This will require you to stay put for at least thirty seconds before you can download the software.

19. After thirty seconds, you will be asked where you want to download the application. You can either request for a code or directly download the software to your unit.

20. Click the "direct download".

21. After clicking, you will see another pop-up window in your Kindle Fire unit, which may state downloading of (specific software), click save or decline.

22. Click "save" and the application will start downloading.

23. After downloading, a notification will display confirming your activity. You can either start using the downloaded kindle fire apps or scan for other applications.

Instructions for http://m.freefireapps.net:
(Note: Make sure that you are connected to a stable wireless fidelity net service connection to download the application without technical problems)

1. Go to your settings and activate your "Wi-Fi search" application.

2. Scan for the available Wi-Fi spot.

3. Connect on it. However, if the available Wi-Fi connection requires a password, then you should type the password first before you will be authenticated and permitted to connect.

4. Once connected, open your kindle fire "internet browser".

5. Key in the given link http://m.freefireapps.net

6. In this site, you will be required to create an account. Unlike with the first site, you need to have an active email address in order to create an official account with this site.

7. Click the "create account" and complete the required information. You will be required to encode your active email address. After setting your account, a notification will display that you need to verify your account through your email address.

8. Check your email and open the message from http://m.freefireapps.net. Click the link at the bottom of the message to finalize the account. This will direct you to the homepage of the website. The purpose of this account is to provide you with newsletters and updates regarding the kindle fire apps available.

9. Ideally, you need to check your email regularly to get updates from this website.

10. When downloading, you just need to follow the same instructions stated in the previous website. The only difference is that you don't need to choose a specific device because this website is exclusive for Kindle Fire units only. Basically, it means that all of the available applications are made

compatible for your Kindle Fire gadget.

While there are many other Android sites out their like the Google play store these two websites are a good place to start looking at for free kindle fire apps. Why not get your gadget out now and start downloading the latest and most popular applications for your kindle fire unit.

FREE KINDLE FIRE PRODUCTIVITY APPS.

Circle Alarm

Circle Alarm is a simple and functional alarm clock. With plenty of functions, the app could be what you need to get up in the morning. With lot of functions, the app has many alarms including vibration mode, recurring alarms and snooze. You can use either the alarm sound of the app or choose your favorite music to wake up to. The volume of the app also increases gradually so you can wake gently.

http://bit.ly/14avPsy

Wunderlist

Wunderlist is a free Kindle app which can be used for organizing your tasks. This is free cloud-sync task manager that allows you to take care of those "to do" lists while you're on the go. For that reason, you should have no problem increasing your productivity rate as soon as you start to use this app.

http://bit.ly/17s8UXw

Timer and Stopwatch

Timer and Stopwatch is a two in one free kindle app that users can use both as an alarm and stopwatch. The timer and stopwatch can be active at the same time.

http://bit.ly/1cAEDvB

Alarm Clock Xtreme

Alarm clock Xtreme is a good free app for any kindle users who wants to wake up gradually. Its alarm increase gradually to give a pleasant wakeup call rather than a sudden loud noise. The app also has a snooze function if you're trying to get another 10 -15 minutes of sleep.

http://bit.ly/13xDeT1

AniFlipClock LITE

AniFlipClock LITE free app is an animated Flip-Clock for Kindle users.

This is the LITE version of the alarm clock with all it functional facilities. The themes of the app are changeable and you can also download themes online. This app always shows hours, minutes, month, and date. It also allows you to change the background colors and designs and has a simple single tap or double tap system to make adjustments.

http://bit.ly/14awme1

FREE KINDLE FIRE GAMING APPS

Green Farm HD

Green Farm is a free Kindle game which is getting more popular every day. This app won't provide you online gaming with other gamers but it has all the other features. You can earn coins in the app and buy upgraded things for your farm including crops, trees, buildings and animals.

http://bit.ly/Hpl8nS

Angry Birds

Who doesn't know about "Angry Birds" at this stage? This is one of those games which always comes packed with lots of different and interesting levels. "It's time to make those bad piggy's pay!"

http://bit.ly/GTK5Y0

Fruit Ninja

Fruit Ninja is another well-known android game which delivers lots to the kindle user. It comes with three different stages including Zen, arcade and classic theme. Slash and carve through piles of fresh fruits in this fun arcade action game. It's important to keep your eyes on the screen at all times and don't miss those super fruits. Different levels and points will reveal better weapons and levels in this game.

http://bit.ly/za9Onz

Triple Town

Triple Town is one of those games that involves building up a city and completing objectives for each level. This slide game is amazing to play and encourages players to think before they build so that they place the right things in the right place at the right time. In this game, you will also face some trouble in the form of bears who come to destroy your city. A fun game for passing the time away.

http://bit.ly/WDgYDO

Dungeon Hunter 3

Dungeon Hunter 3 is the third version of the Dungeon Hunter series and comes with 4 new classes to the users including Warlord, Shaman, Astromancer and Trickster. The main changes in the game are its graphics where it provides great textures and advanced shades with good animation. The powers of evil are growing in Gothicus and it's up to you to sort it out. With 16 different areas full of evil you're going to be very busy.

http://bit.ly/IvrPrd

Airport Mania

In the Airport Mania game, it's your turn to become an air traffic controller. It takes a lot of work to make an airport run smoothly. Whether that's guiding planes in for landing, unloading passengers, repairing refueling it's all go. It going to take skill to coordinate all those take off and landings, are you up to the challenge?

http://bit.ly/11F3b1K

FREE KINDLE FIRE APPS FOR KIDS

AniWorld Lite

AniWorld Lite is a free app for kindle which is developed specially for kids aged one to five years old. This is a cute app to help younger children with learning the names of different animals. They can feed the animals as well as pet them through the apps.

http://bit.ly/16sSaTc

Famigo Sandbox

Famigo Sandbox is a brilliant app for kids that provide a number of free apps inside. Parents can browse through the app selection and choose the right app for their child. For that reason, it's possible to find good and safe apps for kids without specific types of advertising inside. It also provides a section where you can enter the child's kid's age and find apps suit to them.

http://bit.ly/1cATLJi

How to Make Paper Airplanes

How to make paper airplanes has become one the best free apps for children of all ages. The app teaches how to make a paper airplane easily through videos that most kids can following along to. Now, your kids can create some awesome paper airplanes they can be proud of.

http://bit.ly/13xTvHM

Angry Birds Space

Angry Birds Space is another great gaming app that's free for kindle. If you've ever tried any of the other angry bird's game you'll also love this one. This game is perfect for all age groups with plenty of fun and challenges for everyone.

http://bit.ly/1b50J7J

Dabble- The Fast Thinking Word Game

Dabble app is a word thinking game which is perfect for all school going kids. This free app provides lots of great fun and provides kids with a chance to enrich their vocabulary.

http://bit.ly/ljcrmX

The Night Sky

The Night Sky is a free game where kids can learn about satellites and track their movements. The app provides them the names along with details of each satellite. If your child loves everything "spacey" they'll enjoy this app.

http://bit.ly/14smS0N

Real Racing 2

Real Racing 2 is a free app for kindle users which is based on car racing. If your kid loves racing games, real racing is the one for them. There's a great range of car models of car and plenty of tracks to challenge any speed racer.

http://bit.ly/1b50OIl

FREE KINDLE FIRE DRAWING APPS

Sketch n Draw

Sketch n Draw is a free drawing app for kindle users and great for the artist in your home. This app equips the user with 14 different brushes with an eraser and canvas for drawing great images. There are multiple canvas sizes and starts from 240 x 320 to 800 x 1280. The canvas also allows zooming in and out for greater views.

http://bit.ly/GW5CRB

Paint Sparkles Draw - My First Coloring Book HD!

Paint Sparkles Draw is a coloring book with more than 200 coloring pages and makes use of the high definition on the Kindle Fire HD. This drawing app has 11 different categories of images including animals, cars, bikes, and fairies. This app comes with different brush sizes and a fill bucket option to color your pictures.

http://bit.ly/16lOnoO

Paint Joy - Movie Your Drawing

Paint Joy Movie is for kindle app users who love to create fun images. You can choose any type of 20 brushes to paint with, the ability to paint on your existing photos as well as drawing free hand on its canvas. This is a popular drawing app with many more features including different modes of colors, opacity and canvas size. You can draw on the canvas just like a movie and create your own stylish photo very easily.

http://bit.ly/13P8rga

Kaleidoscope Drawing Pad

Kaleidoscope Drawing Pad is a free painting app where Kindle users can use any of six kaleidoscopes for drawing on the canvas. Rainbow, crayon, neon are some of the 10 types of brushes in the app. You can also share your drawings via Gmail and Facebook. Why not create your own magic kaleidoscope drawing today and share it with friends.

http://bit.ly/14VMb4i

Kids Doodle - Movie Kids Drawing

Kid Doodle is an amazing drawing app for the kids. This app has several brushes including rainbow, emboss, neon and so on to paint a great picture. Doodle also allows you the ability to paint any picture and save it to your kindle. This drawing options is easy for young children to master and use.

http://bit.ly/14KwPUe

Draw Something

Draw something is a well-known drawing app which is also an online gaming app. Players have to draw images for others who try to work out what the image is. The app has many various kinds of brushes for creating good quality images with plenty of colors to choose from.

http://bit.ly/JnBZgc

Fun Face Changer Extreme

Fun Face Changer Extreme is a drawing app where you can add many things to your existing photos. This is a fun app where you can lots of fun things onto people's faces or dress up images by using the tools of the app. To use the app on your Kindle, you need to choose any photo and chose which stickers you want to use. You can resize the stickers by using your finger on the screen and adjust it on photos easily. The cool stickers come with different features to provide fun including animal heads, different hair styles, eyes of different types as well as mouth and noses.

http://bit.ly/16Un2tJ

FREE KINDLE FIRE PUZZLE APPS

Where's My Water?

Where's My Water? - is a famous free puzzle app for Kindle users where they have to solve the puzzle to reach the next level. Each of the levels comes with various different challenge for the user. This puzzle gaming app has 100 levels where "Swampy" the crocodile has to supply water to fill his bath. The aim of the game is you solve the puzzles and blockages to supply the water to Swampy. With regular updates it's a game that's will give hours of fun.

http://bit.ly/yiudYl

4 Pics 1 Word Puzzle

4 Pics 1 Word Puzzle is a gaming app where you will get 4 Pics in each level. The pictures will indicate one word and give you hints to work out what the word is. You just need to think about the pictures and chose the word that matches all 4 pictures to reach the next level. By clicking each of the pictures, you can zoom in and out to understand the picture better. This app has also an option to purchase credits to get more game features.

http://bit.ly/16lPwwo

Magic Puzzles

Magic Puzzles is a good puzzle game for the Kindle and comes with 4 different levels. It comes with 42 pieces, 72 pieces, 143 pieces and 288 pieces for you to play with. Each puzzle must be solved to reach next level of the game. This app has many different themes including nature and animals.

http://bit.ly/17sjjTd

Words with Friends

Words with Friends is also a puzzle game where you can share your puzzles and words with your friends. Moreover, in this app, you can play multiple people for more fun and to make it more challenging. This is a fun and addictive word game that will also help to enrich your vocabulary. http://bit.ly/xvYQHN

Mind Games

Mind games is a type of brain training exercising games with 17 levels. Each of the levels will test your brain and give your percentage ranking after each level. It has 17 different brain exercising games for you with history to record your progress. So, why not get your brain down to the gym today?

http://bit.ly/15Fjuwd

FREE KINDLE FIRE READING APPS

Adobe Digital Editions

Adobe Digital Editions is a popular eBook reader for kindle users that allows the users to open PDF and EPUB files. The reading view has some external features, which allow you to bookmark any page and the option of annotations and view the table of contents. It also allows you to hide its navigation menu and view the book in wide screen.

http://adobe.ly/1xNv

Sony Reader Library

Sony Reader Library is a free kindle eBook reader, which can be used for reading documents. This app can open PDF, TXT, DOC, EPUB as well as other files on your kindle. This app can import files from the Sony Reader Library as well as download them directly from the website. This Sony library store has many books for sale with an RSS feed option for users.

http://bit.ly/UcXuWP

Barnes and Nobile Nook Apps

The Barnes and Nobile Nook reading app is free for the Kindle fire as it is for many other devices. The app opens up the ability to access B&N's online bookstore and download books from there. However, to download books from the website you will need to become a member of the website.

http://bit.ly/16lRRaC

MobiPocket Reader

MobiPocket Reader is a free Kindle document reader app, which supports MOBIE and PRC eBooks. MobiPocket official websites has more than 40,000 book titles which are available for download.

Modifying font size and type, changing your reading view, editing page size and changing the display colors are some of the great features of this app. In addition, it provides an English dictionary to search up any word to understand its meaning.

http://bit.ly/dPiGP

Microsoft Reader

The Microsoft reader is a free app for reading your documents. As soon as you enter into the app, you will need to register the app to view any eBooks. Microsoft boasts has more than 60,000 titles, which you can easily download from their server free of cost.

http://cnet.co/v05xvi

Free Books for Kindle

If you're looking for free books, Free Books for Kindle could be just the app you've been looking for. Just use the search option and you can find thousands of books for each search. You can get many books free of cost through the app and also receive free notifications when any new books become available.

http://bit.ly/12S4ahO

Stanza Desktop

Stanza Desktop is a free eBook reader for Kindle users that comes with different features including text scrolling, font size change, change font color, change font size; create new layouts and so on. This app supports most files including PDF, HTML, DOC, and RTF.

http://bit.ly/69QCV4

ComiCat

Are you searching for a free Kindle comic reader app? Then, download ComiCat app now for reading all your digital comics on your Kindle. This app allows the user to read CBR and CBZ files as well as a catalogue of comics.

http://bit.ly/19G6aMo

ComiXology

ComiXology comic reader is a free app for kindle that has some great features for users. This reader allows the support of increasing font size and navigation.

http://bit.ly/wctkfK

Perfect Viewer

Perfect Viewer may not be the first choice for reading comics in your Kindle but it has some features, which are so important. This app can support a large number of formats of comics including PNG, BMP, JPEG, Lahr, PDF files and so on.

http://amzn.to/NrwfE8

Readability

Readability app is a neat little app that allows you to read any Web page now or save it for reading later on. By using the Readability "add on" on your browser you can catch up on reading this content later on your kindle. This app is great for giving you a better reading view that's tidier with the ability to read your web content whenever you like without disturbance. You can also customize the text's size and font color to make reading easier.

http://bit.ly/13d63AG

FREE KINDLE FIRE WEIGHT LOSS AND FITNESS APPS

Lose It!

Lose It is a great app for anyone looking to lose weight. To use it simply type in your details like how much weight you want to lose and the app creates a weight loss program for you. This is a great app for recording your calorie count and has tons of common place meals, foods and restaurants so you always know how many calories you're eating. You can also connect to others so you're never too far from a weight loss buddy. Give it a go you've nothing to lose except body fat!

http://bit.ly/HokBbd

Calorie Counter – MyFitnessPal

Calorie Count-My Fitness Pal is as the name suggests a calorie counter. Packed with over 3,000,000 (yes that's 3 million) foods and the calories they contain this is a great tool to have in your weight loss arsenal. The app also includes more than 350 exercise and training sessions, this could be just what your body has been looking for.

http://bit.ly/ONsBpH

Daily Workouts

Daily Workouts is a free app for Kindle users, which provides workout information and how to do them. This workout app allows the user to select from between 5 to 30 minutes workouts depending on their fitness levels. This app has about 50 different exercises along with videos showing how to do each workout. The app also comes with a timer and on screen instruction so you always know what to do.

http://bit.ly/13Pufbj

Simply Yoga

Simple Yoga is an ad free app that as the name suggests helps you to learn yoga. The app comes with different levels of workout from a 20, 40 and 60-minute workout with video. All videos are demonstrated by a certified yoga instructor so you're never left wondering what to do. So if you've always wanted to give yoga a go but was putting it off this could be just what you've been looking for.

http://bit.ly/1elqD70

Workout Trainer

Workout Trainer is a free app for Kindle users to help them out at workout time. Packed with lots of trainers that give proper instruction through audio and video they lots that you can do. Whether that's a fitness goal like weight loss, more flexibility, creating a 6-pack abs and so on you'll find lots of great fitness content here.

http://bit.ly/S3p4mt

FREE KINDLE FIRE HD PHOTO APPS

Pic Collage

Pic Collage is a free photo app for the Kindle fire HD, which allows you to capture and view any photo available in your album. You can rotate the photos easily with your two fingers and delete with the quick delete option. You can also change the color of your photo and use text with different font styles and size. This is the all in one app where you can capture your photo, use instant edit to edit and rotate and then share it on Facebook.

http://amzn.to/18WHBbi

Photo Editor

Photo Editor is a simple and easy app for Kindle Fire HD for photo capturing, viewing as well as editing. With Photo Editor you can adjust the pictures color, rotating your picture, and add effects to your photos. With the high demand for photo editing as soon as it's captured, this app is one of the best choice for Kindle HD users to get all. This app includes 125 unique filters in different editing categories.

http://bit.ly/1c0e7Og

Photo Studio

Photo Studio is an awesome free app for any android device as well as the Kindle Fire HD for capturing professional photos at any moment. Photographers can take a simple image but using the power of this great app you can make your snap even sharper with better quality. Any user can capture a photo and with their Kindle Fire HD have a great photo studio right at their fingertips.

http://bit.ly/192bt9F

Picasa

Picasa is one of the more famous and free photos capturing as well as photo editing apps for Kindle Fire HD as well as other devices. This app comes with menu bar in which the user can find different types of features including background change, photo from gallery mode, load photos, and instant editing of pictures. Then users can easily share their edited photos instantly via Face book, Email and Twitter.

http://bit.ly/14b5Otj

FREE KINDLE FIRE MUSIC APPS

SoundHound

Sound Hound is a free music app for the Kindle Fire users who love to listen music on it. This app is available in most of the websites of kindle apps free of cost. The app can easily recognize music very quickly and also show you the lyrics of the song. This app is also connected with many social networks including Facebook, YouTube, twitter where you can directly share the song.

http://bit.ly/IrolJI

TuneIn Radio

Tunnel Radio allows the user to listen to radio channels from all over the world. In addition, this app also be used for listening to music and songs whenever you want. With this music app, you can enjoy more than 70,000 live radio stations and podcasts from all over the world as well as open music with it.

http://bit.ly/xK8pJp

SoundCloud

Sound Cloud is an app for listening to new fresh and free music tracks on your Kindle. Sound Cloud is one of the largest communities for the musicians and bands where new music is constantly being uploaded. With this app you can play music directly from the cloud. With features like the ability to record your own voice as well as share songs and lyrics via Google+ and Facebook. This could quickly become one of your favorite apps.

http://bit.ly/T1leHi

8Tracks Radio

8Tracks Radio is a radio and music app for Kindle, which can provide great music according to your own personal taste. This is free app without any audio ads or limits that some other music apps have. 8Tracks Radio also allows you to listen to any song and make your own playlists. The app can categorize the music according to rock, jazz and classical automatically. So, what are you waiting for go and join the other 5 million listeners that you use 8Tracks Radio every month.

http://bit.ly/JU20TD

Digital Pan

How would you like to have you own steel drum on your Kindle Fire? Now's your chance with "Digital Pan" which is free to Kindle users. With lots of features including a steel drum that you can happily play along on it might just become your new pastime? In addition, you can also keep a recording of your favorites for whenever you want to play your music.

http://bit.ly/183fh63

Music Web Browser

Music Web Browser is new and widely used app for Kindle Fire and android users to search out the newest music and songs. With this web browser, the users can bookmark their favorite music websites and favorite music hangouts. This app allows you to get direct access to the many streaming music websites online and also online radio websites to enjoy free music. Users can get direct access to many music websites and search any artists or album within only a few seconds.

http://bit.ly/1b5cNpz

FREE KINDLE FIRE FOOD APPS

Giant Food Healthy Ideas

Giant Food Healthy Ideas is a great food app for the Kindle and android users which is free to download. This is a popular app, which always give lots of healthy foods tips, advice and money saving tips. Like the magazine, the app also provides useful news and ideas to help you to a healthier life. The professionals of food health topic always work for getting the newest news about food and highlight to them.

http://bit.ly/1elsFnn

Stop & Shop Healthy Ideas

Stop & Shop Healthy Ideas is the app for the people who loves to cook for themselves and their loved ones. This free food recipe maker app has plenty of recipes to you according to your taste and has lots of advice and suggestions from health professional to ensure your healthy lifestyle.

http://bit.ly/183fANW

Martin's Healthy Ideas

Martin's Healthy Ideas is both healthy and food app frees for the android phones as well as Kindle users. This is the app, which is full of ideas and suggestions for a good health and makes a good choice for your family to lead healthy life.

Each of the issue and healthy chapter has wide verity of health suggestions, recipes, and friendly to shopping ideas as well as ideas about the food. Most of the recipes are invented for those users who used to lead a healthy life for them. The suggestions always provide good action and ideas for the users, which is dependent.

http://bit.ly/15Fxbvp

FREE KINDLE FIRE WEATHER APPS

WeatherBug

WeatherBug is one of the best and world's largest network for forecasting the weather of any city or country. When you download this app on your Kindle free you can keep up to date on the latest weather with alerts for any bad weather coming your way. With easy to use side slide navigation and the ability to customize backgrounds plus a more than 25% better accurate weather forecast than other services this app may quickly become your touchstone before you leave the house in the morning.

http://bit.ly/zfaIa0

NewsHog: Google News & Weather

NewsHog is listed by USA Today as one of the top 25 must have apps for the Kindle Fire and gives its users the latest news and weather forecasts. All news and weather comes from Googles aggregated service so you'll always have the latest news and weather on your NewsHog newsreader.

http://bit.ly/1b5d7oi

MyExtras

MyExtras is all in one app for the Kindle user including daily weather forecast news, entertainment and horoscopes for you. The app updates daily provide all the latest weather forecasts and daily horoscope. In fact, this app gives a 10-day weather forecast news with radar maps so you'll always know in advance what the weather is going to be like in your city. Also apart from weather, horoscopes and news MyExtra is well worth installing as its packed with lots of daily tips, freebies and discounts on products and services.

http://bit.ly/15v2gUX

RECOMMENDED READING

Finally, while I may feel I've provided you with lots of great tips, tricks and ways to get more from your kindle fire. I'd be amiss to not recommend other great kindle fire books. Here are my top 3…

Kindle Fire Tips & Tricks - Tim Sievers

http://amzn.to/1b5duPq

Kindle Fire Tips, Tricks and Traps: A How-To Tutorial for the Kindle Fire HD – Edward Jones

http://amzn.to/1cpgSlm

Secret Kindle Fire Tips & Tricks – Gadget

http://amzn.to/15v4Fit